Let Me Let Go

poems by

Jennifer Davis Michael

Finishing Line Press
Georgetown, Kentucky

Let Me Let Go

Copyright © 2020 by Jennifer Davis Michael
ISBN 978-1-64662-116-3 First Edition
All rights reserved under International and Pan-American Copyright Conventions. No part of this book may be reproduced in any manner whatsoever without written permission from the publisher, except in the case of brief quotations embodied in critical articles and reviews.

ACKNOWLEDGMENTS

I'm very grateful to the editors of the following journals where these poems first appeared, some in earlier versions:

3Elements Review: "Spiderweb"
Amsterdam Quarterly: "Family Music"
Cumberland River Review: "Last Afternoon at the Beach"
Leaping Clear: "Annie and Lucy"
Literary Mama: "Each of His Cries Is a Different Color"
Magnolia Review: "Remembering How to Build a Fire"
Mezzo Cammin: "Cicadas" and "The God of Things That Are Not"
New Verse News: "Border Guard" (under the title "The Border Far Away")
Pine Mountain Sand & Gravel: "After the Bypass"
Silver Birch Press "Beach & Pool Memories" Series: "Opening the Hand" (under the title "First Taste of the Sublime")
Southern Poetry Review: "Meridian"
Switchgrass Review: "Maiden Aunt" and "Produce"
Think: "Premonition"

Deepest thanks also to Leigh Anne Couch, who helped this book find its shape, and to Virginia Craighill, David Landon, and Luann Landon for their critical insights and fellowship.

Publisher: Leah Maines
Editor: Christen Kincaid
Cover Art: Jennifer Davis Michael
Author Photo: Buck Butler
Cover Design: Elizabeth Maines McCleavy

Printed in the USA on acid-free paper.
Order online: www.finishinglinepress.com
also available on amazon.com

Author inquiries and mail orders:
Finishing Line Press
P. O. Box 1626
Georgetown, Kentucky 40324
U. S. A.

Table of Contents

Opening the Hand 1

First Death 2

Down the Hall 3

Meridian 4

Maiden Aunt 5

After the Bypass 6

Family Music 7

Firefly Time 8

Spiderweb 9

Tosca at the Piggly Wiggly 10

Produce 11

The God of Things That Are Not 12

Premonition 13

Weight 14

Cicadas 15

Annie and Lucy 16

Each of His Cries Is a Different Color 17

Border Guard 18

Maple Tree on Fire 19

Remembering How to Build a Fire 20

Stroke 21

Packing the Black Dress 22

Last Afternoon at the Beach 23

*For my family,
given and found*

Opening the Hand

I don't recall my first view of the beach:
my terror at the blank expanse of sand
and that tremendous, always-moving water.
No silent-movie footage of me bolting
for the motel's sliding door or burying
my face in my father's scratchy neck.
But there's a photo of my hooded self,
snug, smiling in the nest he dug for me:
a tiny sea enclosed by shoveled walls
—infinity made comprehensible.

I do remember two or three years later,
he took me in the surf up to his waist
and taught me how to float there, on my back.
The water chilled my ears and muted sounds,
so that I felt the waves but didn't hear them.
His hand stayed on my shoulder
until a gust of wind blew off his cap
and he lunged, letting go of me. Just then
an upstart wave, whipped up by that same wind,
broke over me. I choked and came up crying,
cursing him in the wordless way of children,
but he was there. He'd never been away.
And yet, in that split-second of emptiness,
by opening his hand, he'd let me feel the sea.

First Death

Home from preschool, hand on the door,
I looked down to a flash of blue
spilled like silk on the dull gravel.
Indigo bunting, my mother said,
and then another word, *dead*.
We found a shoebox (my Buster Browns
about his size) and nested him
with tissue paper, as if to cushion
his final landing. I don't recall
who dug the hole, or if I cried.
I do know this was the first.
A piece of sky had come to earth,
and tenderness and ritual
are all the answers that we have.

Down the Hall

I am going down the hall
in my childhood house.
Our father has summoned
my brother and me.
It feels like a dream, and not.
The hall seems shorter,
ceilings lower.
I let my brother go first,
though I was first. We pass
his bedroom door, then mine,
the photos in their frames.
At the end is our father's bed.
He has things to say,
not yet the last things
and yet the movement feels
like last, and first,
down the hall,
a narrowing space.
I will be here again,
and soon.
Down the hall.
My father calls.

Meridian

Red light stops us under the overpass:
satellite radio drops into silence,
the strange percussion of traffic above.

At the auto parts store (closed for the night)
the balloon man performs his spastic dance
to the unheard music of lost connections.

Light changed, we edge toward the cracked ramp
as the oldies station roars back to life.
Rising, we join the irregular vibration.

Maiden Aunt

"Different" in ways no one could quite explain,
unfit for school by skill or disposition,
uninterested in boys and their smooth lines,
she dodged our bookish family's expectations,
embracing tasks we viewed as menial:
changing diapers and wiping noses
of children not her blood, but all her own.

Yet no one set more store by family:
the birthday parties, minor holidays,
rituals of baking and the handmade gift,
the store-bought card with the most cloying words
underlined twice or thrice in ballpoint pen.
She doted on her niece and nephew,
making up pet names that embarrassed them,
buying them toys and clothes a shade too young.

Those other children she had raised adored her
from afar: their letters bustling with news
and snaggle-toothed school photos tucked inside,
all to be passed around at family meals.
And after supper, when we talked of books,
she would fade into a corner of the porch
to knit a blanket or to rock a child.
Occasionally we'd hear her hum or sing
an old song from her teenage years, as if
she'd tuned into a distant radio,
a song that none of us could hear.

After the Bypass

After the bypass, they stapled him shut,
a scar like a railroad down his chest.
Home alone, he measured time
by pills and heartbeats.

One morning the phone rang through the haze.
Pharmacy? Hospital? Only later
his clearing mind caught. "Catherine's daughter," she'd said.
Your daughter, she meant, but couldn't speak
the word to connect the crossties.
"Asheville." Or "Nashville." Her accent was thick
as the fog in his ears. Silence rattled his chest.
She never called back.

So he bought a truck
and painted his heart on the side,
"John Smith, Seeking Daughter," in red.
He drives through the towns
where he thinks she might be,
parks at intersections,
then sleeps in motels with the TV on low,
awaiting her call. But mostly what he hears
is the train whistle blowing a path through the dark
from one town's vague border to the next.

Family Music

We sleep chastely at your parents' house:
you in the basement, full of silent history,
I among the relics of your boyhood.
Tonight, I lie awake under a quilt
stitched by hands I will never know.

I listen to the household symphony:
you and your mother doing the cooks' dance,
your sister showering before her graveyard shift,
dog and baby pattering staccato on the floor,
ignoring papa's deep-voiced directions.

I hear this music only from backstage.
To hear it is to know, not them, but you
—my new love, bringer of strange melodies—
as I drift to sleep here in your childhood bed,
alone but wrapped in a seductive tune.

Firefly Time

We walked home at firefly time.
Crepuscular concupiscence
charged the dim air with energy,
blurring the crisp suburban lawns.
The trees were darker than the sky,
their outlines liquefying.
Deer stood like the pause at the top of a breath.

And all around, fireflies
cast their lusty lantern beams,
oblivious to us.

Desire hangs at the margins
of light and darkness, life and death.
We hover on the threshold,
blinking a code we barely know.

But I spoke none of that. Instead,
my hand swam toward your unseen hand.
Arriving home, we switched on lights
just long enough to find our way upstairs.

Spiderweb

We lingered on the porch long after dark,
as bats flapped softly far above our heads,
cicadas swelled their rasping symphony,
and fireflies punctuated evening's fall.

Silhouetted by the kitchen's glazed light,
a spider hung between the house and railing
amid the tattered remnants of a web.
We watched as she consumed the broken silk,
erasing her old handiwork, until
only a single, anchor thread remained.
She then began to chart a pattern known
to her alone until she finished it.
 "How does she know . . . " I murmured,
and left the question dangling.

We quietly cheered when she completed it,
as proud as if she'd been our child—
not thinking of the flies or moths
who'd also be enthralled by her dark art.
Conspirators, we tiptoed in the house,
walking on sticky lines spun long ago:
resilient, intricate, too large to see.

Tosca at the Piggly Wiggly

Outside the Piggly Wiggly,
in the flooded parking lot,
I wait out the storm in the car,
the radio tuned to *Tosca*.

Just then a woman bursts
from a red pickup, unprotected,
head bowed against the shower,
ill-fitting jeans soaked indigo
above flip-flops. Her jaw is set.
She clutches a vinyl purse.

At the filling station across the lot,
a girl who looks fourteen
stands smoking beside a gas pump.
She reads my stare and scowls.

As Tosca takes her plunge,
the rain grows bored and slackens.
For art, for love, for treachery,
the groceries can wait.

Produce

They nearly block the produce aisle:
an older man in overalls,
a teenage girl, and two small kids,
one lolling in the shopping cart.
The other, darting in and out between
the overflowing sale displays—
bananas sixty cents a pound,
peanuts to shell yourself, Corn Flakes—
grabs not fruit, but some manmade
facsimile: Fruit by the Foot. No need
to touch the box to feel its stickiness,
to taste the stale, unsatisfying sweet.

His sister (or is she his mom?)
sees my impatience, tells him to move.
The gray-haired man, oblivious,
peruses iceberg lettuce, picks a head.
That's when the youngest, in the cart,
turns my way, clutching a makeshift pack
of ice against her face, a grape-red bruise
blooming across her cheek. I stare,
not meaning to. The sister-mom meets my gaze
deliberately. "She fell off her bike."

Of course. And who'd think otherwise?
And why do you assume I would
because I'm wearing L. L. Bean?
But all I say is, "Yes, I see she did,"
and to the child, "I'm sure that hurts."
Her face, though scraped, is closed to me
as I pass, chastened, as if I
had something to feel guilty for.
Ahead, there's pomegranate juice
and jellies in expensive jars.

The God of Things That Are Not

Across a crowded dinner table,
plates full and glasses charged,
a friend tells me a new name for God:
The God of Things That Are Not.

My mind needs space to picture these:
vases empty, voices stilled,
the crumbs swept from the table. And here he comes:
a God who gathers up the unused dishes,

who cherishes the things undone,
the phone call not returned,
the breakfast skipped, the blank page,
photographs snapped with lens cap on.

And that which is not finds a home
in the margins of abundance,
between one feast of being and the next,
in space that only seems unfilled.

Premonition

I could not dream your birth (a thing unknown)
but dreamed your presence, inexplicable:
a nest for you beside me in the bed.
Days afterward you swam from me too soon
into the grasp of metal, glare of lights,
the hands of those who knew things I did not.
Now, as you find your footing in the world,
on squally nights I dream of losing you
around a corner, in a street, a forest.
Most often, it's in water:
you just beyond my reach, the water black,
my limbs weak as a newborn's, my voice
half strangled, as you slip out of the light
the way you first slid out of me, too soon.

Weight

I knew your measure, weightless in my womb,
your quickening in the quickness of my pulse.
At birth you shed this cumbersome abode
for compact, naked elegance: four pounds.

My body learned to measure you again
from the outside: your ear against my heart,
mouth pulling at my breast, the tiny hand
gripping my finger with astonishing force.

My heart burst from my ribs and had to find
another home: it tried to fit itself
around you, keeps stretching as you grow:
your fists beating against its supple walls.

Now, balancing your own weight on your legs,
you size up distances, intuiting
the physics of your separateness from me,
denouncing gravity and finitude.

Late heavy nights, I wait as your cries build,
then rock your howling energy in my arms,
feeling your flesh sink into mine again
as, one by one, our terrors fall asleep.

Each of His Cries Is a Different Color

His first cry: a thin pale blue
as he flopped like a fish from sea to land,
then purple as he moored his breath
and fought his helpers' tools and hands.
His sleepy cry is green as grass
nibbled by those elusive sheep.
Hunger, bright orange—a burning sun
needs constant fuel to stoke its flames
—but not as bright as pain, white-hot,
a blinding flash across his name.
His angry cry runs red as blood:
the voice of raw humanity
protesting all that is not right
with tears enough to salt the sea.

Cicadas

Their song, pulsating, punctuates
the feverish July afternoon.
Like wine, it's been cellared in the earth,
building in body and complexity,
as the nymph eats and grows, shrugging loose
one skin after another: tissue-like tunnels
inside the earthen tunnel where it feeds.
At last it climbs from darkness into day,
hidden music unfolding from below.
The singers leave behind a shell of song,
translucent husks clinging to bark,
which my three-year-old collects with delight,
lining them on the steps in mute parade
as the choir crescendos overhead.

Annie and Lucy

Before, you swam entwined.
Now in your separate nests,
sprung too soon,
enclosed in plexiglass,
you grasp the feeding tubes
with absolute possession.
Machines hum lullabies.
Green numbers, blinking lights
your bedtime story.
Not as your parents wished it,
as they sit, shocked and drained,
thinking of home, the pink nursery waiting.
No, but it is your story,
one you will tell each other
late nights under the covers,
years from now:
how the two of you leapt
from heaven, and the startled world
held out its arms and caught you.

Border Guard

My son is white like me, the border far away.
According to his papers and my scar
where forceps dragged him earthward, he is mine.
We don't discuss what's happening down there
—I mean, down at the border. He's just six.
He's learning how to swim. A patient guard
shapes his flailing dog-paddle to a stroke
that might cross rivers. She lightly pins his feet
to bend his body to a diving arc.

"Far away from home, it looks like darkness":
his random comment on the vegetation
we speed past on the way back from the pool.
He sleeps that night, surfacing only once
from nightmares of the house crumbling around us.
I guard the borders of his innocence,
my trigger-finger on the remote control.

Maple Tree on Fire

Outside the café window,
a maple tree on fire:
wrung dry by drought
and lit by late rain.
Inside, the *whoosh* of espresso;
smoky soul music,
"Let me let go."

Last week, my father in this same café,
unsteady with his cane,
jostling the table, spilling coffee:
the waitress bustling over,
Dad lifting the cup to help,
tipping it onto his shirt,
her fussing, fretting, blotting him
with that damp gray rag.
I met the milk-froth pity in her voice
with anger spilling over,
scalding me.

Today, thinking of my father
and that maple tree on fire,
I lift the cup deliberately,
drink with care.

Remembering How to Build a Fire

Crumple exactly four sheets of newsprint.
Arrange them sentry-like across the floor
of the stove. Brace front and back with larger logs.
Criss-cross with kindling (prefer sassafras).
Touch match to paper. Wait for it to catch.

For twenty years I've only had gas logs
—much cleaner, more convenient. But my dad
long ago taught me the art of building fires,
shaping combustion with an architect's hand,
a pattern soon resolving heat to ash.

Be careful not to build the fire too high.
Leave the stove door ajar to help it draw
the smoke. Now sit and watch the crackling dance,
the living core of home and heart:
the edifice that must destroy itself.

These days, my father can't remember much.
His mind tunes in and out, a radio
dialed slightly off the station. Once again
I'm crouching next to him beside the hearth,
eyes stinging as the damp wood smolders down.

Stroke

The way time creeps
in a hospital room
at two-thirty p.m.
when it's rained all day
and the room is hot
and the windows don't open.

The way his head
is turned toward you
even though his eyes
are closed, even though
it's because of the stroke
that he's turned this way.

The way the grip
is still so strong
in his right hand,
the one that works,
that won't let go
when you try to leave.

The way time halts
after galloping past
for forty-nine years
and especially
the last twenty-five.
The way the clock strikes.

Packing the Black Dress

Black dress, black tights, and closed-toed shoes:
I take them on each trip with me,
not knowing when my dad will loose

himself from muscles he can't use,
the daily loss of dignity.
Black dress, black tights, and closed-toed shoes:

that's what I'll need to wear, when news
breaks that he's gone. I wait to see
what piece of him is next to lose

its function. Whether I would choose
this state for him is not for me
to say. I look down at my shoes

while he speaks of escape, some ruse
to fool the nurses and get free.
How little he has left to lose.

Dementia is its own excuse.
I pack my outfit carefully:
black dress, black tights, and closed-toed shoes.
The bag is full; my grip is loose.

Last Afternoon at the Beach

The sand grows golden with the sinking sun,
and footprints slowly fill with shadows.
Men and women, crusted with sweat
and sunscreen, bend to fold their chairs,
shake off the accumulated grains of the day:
moments caught through salt-blurred lenses.
Children straggle up from the ebbing tide,
chafed by sun, wind, and admonitions.
Their buckets clink with shells,
smelling of salty decay.
Next year they will be older, less in awe
of the sublime reach that pulls, gives back,
pulls and gives back. This day,
so fresh and clean at its unfurling, darts
like a ghost crab past the corner of your eye.

Jennifer Davis Michael grew up beside a lake in Auburn, Alabama. She attended Oxford as a Rhodes Scholar and holds a doctorate from Northwestern University. Since 1995 she has taught English literature, primarily British Romanticism, at the University of the South in Sewanee, Tennessee, where she earned her B.A. Her monograph *Blake and the City* was published by Bucknell University Press in 2006. *Let Me Let Go* was a finalist in the Comstock Writers' Group Chapbook Contest. Her poems have appeared in print journals such as *Think, Switchgrass Review, Southern Poetry Review,* and *The Windhover,* and in online journals such as *Literary Mama, Cumberland River Review, 3Elements Review, The Amethyst Review, The Magnolia Review, Turtle Island Quarterly, Poetry24, The New Verse News, Poets Reading the News, Amsterdam Quarterly, Leaping Clear, Mezzo Cammin,* and *District Lit.* Her poem "Bell of Silence," set to music by her brother, Nathan Davis, was commissioned for performance by the Park Avenue Christian Church in New York City. She is married to Jim Pappas, an Episcopal priest, and they have a young son.

www.ingramcontent.com/pod-product-compliance
Lightning Source LLC
LaVergne TN
LVHW050046090426
835510LV00043B/3334